HOW TO FISH FOR LARGEMOUTH BASS IN LAKES

Johnson Wu

A Practical Guide to Techniques, Tactics, and Gear

ISBN 978-1-998455-93-5 (Paperback)
ISBN 978-1-998455-94-2 (eBook)

Printed and bound in USA
Published by Loons Press

Table Of Contents

How To Fish For Largemouth Bass In Lakes

A Practical Guide to Techniques, Tactics, and Gear

Chapter 1

Introduction to Largemouth Bass Fishing

Understanding Largemouth Bass

Largemouth bass (Micropterus salmoides) are one of the most sought-after freshwater fish species in North America, renowned for their aggressive feeding behavior and challenging fight. They inhabit a variety of freshwater environments, including lakes, rivers, and reservoirs, making them accessible to anglers across different regions.

Understanding the biology, behavior, and habitat preferences of largemouth bass is essential for successful fishing. These fish thrive in warm waters, typically ranging from 65°F to 85°F (18°C to 29°C) and are often found in areas with ample cover, such as submerged vegetation, fallen trees, and rocky structures.

The physical characteristics of largemouth bass contribute to their popularity among anglers. They possess a large mouth that extends beyond their eyes, which aids in their predatory nature. Adult largemouth bass can weigh anywhere from 1 to 10 pounds, with some trophy specimens exceeding 20 pounds. Their coloration typically includes dark green or black on the back, fading to lighter shades on the belly, often adorned with a distinctive lateral stripe. This color pattern allows them to blend seamlessly into their surroundings, making them adept ambush predators.

Feeding habits of largemouth bass are influenced by various factors, including time of day, season, and water temperature. They are opportunistic feeders, consuming a diet primarily composed of smaller fish, amphibians, and invertebrates. During warmer months, largemouth bass are most active during dawn and dusk, making these times ideal for anglers. They exhibit a behavior known as "bedding" during the spawning season, which typically occurs in spring when water temperatures rise. Understanding these patterns can significantly enhance an angler's chances of success.

The habitat preferences of largemouth bass are crucial for targeting them effectively. They favor shallow waters with plenty of cover, which provides both protection from predators and ambush points for hunting. Structure such as weed beds, stumps, and docks attract baitfish, making these areas prime locations for fishing. Largemouth bass tend to be more aggressive in warmer months when they are actively feeding, and anglers should focus on areas with varying depths and ample cover to increase their chances of hooking a big catch.

In addition to knowing the fish's habits and habitats, selecting the right gear and techniques is vital for successful largemouth bass fishing. Rod and reel combinations need to be sturdy yet sensitive, allowing anglers to detect subtle bites. Baits can range from live minnows to artificial lures, with topwater lures and soft plastics being particularly effective.

Learning to adapt techniques based on environmental conditions and understanding the behavior of largemouth bass will ultimately lead to a more rewarding fishing experience. Emphasizing knowledge and skill in these areas will empower anglers to master the art of fishing for largemouth bass in lakes.

Introduction of Largemouth Bass in Fishing

This book serves as a comprehensive resource for anglers who wish to enhance their skills in fishing for one of North America's most popular freshwater species. With its distinct fighting ability and varied habitats, largemouth bass present a unique challenge that appeals to both novice and experienced fishermen. This guide aims to equip readers with essential knowledge and practical strategies to successfully locate and catch largemouth bass in lake environments.

The first section of the book delves into understanding the biology and behavior of largemouth bass. By exploring their feeding patterns, spawning cycles, and habitat preferences, readers will gain insights into when and where to find these fish. This foundational knowledge is crucial for developing effective fishing strategies. The book emphasizes the importance of adapting to seasonal changes and water conditions, which can significantly impact bass behavior and, consequently, fishing success.

Next, the guide covers various fishing techniques tailored specifically for largemouth bass. From traditional methods like baitcasting and spinning to modern approaches such as using topwater lures or drop-shot rigs, the book provides detailed explanations and step-by-step instructions. Each technique is accompanied by practical tips, ensuring that anglers can select the best method for their skill level and the specific conditions they encounter. This section empowers readers to experiment with different techniques, enhancing their overall fishing experience.

In addition to techniques, the book emphasizes the importance of using the right gear. An entire chapter is dedicated to selecting rods, reels, lines, and lures that are best suited for targeting largemouth bass. The author discusses the advantages of various materials and designs, helping readers make informed choices based on their personal preferences and budget. Understanding gear not only improves fishing performance but also fosters a deeper appreciation for the sport.

Finally, the book concludes with insights into local regulations and conservation practices, encouraging responsible fishing. As anglers seek to enjoy their time on the water, it is vital to understand the impact of fishing practices on bass populations and aquatic ecosystems. The guide promotes sustainable fishing habits, ensuring that future generations can enjoy the thrill of catching largemouth bass in lakes. By the end of this book, readers will be well-equipped with the knowledge and skills necessary to become proficient in fishing for largemouth bass, making every trip to the lake a rewarding experience.

How To Fish For Largemouth Bass In Lakes

Chapter 2

Essential Gear for Largemouth Bass Fishing

Fishing Rods and Reels

Fishing rods and reels are essential components in the pursuit of largemouth bass, as they significantly influence your success on the water. The right combination can enhance your casting accuracy, improve your lure presentation, and provide the necessary strength to handle larger fish.

When selecting a fishing rod, consider the material, length, and action. Graphite rods are popular for their sensitivity and lightweight design, while fiberglass rods offer durability and strength. A medium to medium-heavy action rod in the range of 6 to 7 feet is generally recommended for bass fishing, as it provides a good balance between casting distance and control.

When it comes to reels, anglers typically choose between spinning reels and baitcasting reels. Spinning reels are user-friendly and ideal for beginners, allowing for smooth casting and easy retrieval of lures. They are particularly effective for finesse techniques, where subtle presentations are key. On the other hand, baitcasting reels offer greater control over line management and are preferred by more experienced anglers targeting larger bass with heavier lures. Understanding the mechanics of each reel type will help you choose the one that best fits your fishing style and techniques.

Line selection is another critical aspect of your fishing rod and reel setup. For largemouth bass, braided line is often favored for its strength and sensitivity, allowing anglers to feel even the lightest bites. Fluorocarbon line is also popular due to its low visibility underwater, making it an excellent choice for clear water conditions. Monofilament line can be used for topwater fishing due to its buoyancy, but it may not perform as well in terms of sensitivity compared to the other options. Matching your line choice with the rod and reel will create an efficient setup for catching bass.

Proper maintenance of your fishing rods and reels is vital for ensuring longevity and optimal performance. After each fishing trip, it's important to clean your gear to remove dirt, salt, and grime that can cause wear over time. Regularly check the guides on your rod for any damage and ensure that your reel is properly lubricated to prevent corrosion. Taking the time to care for your equipment will enhance your fishing experience and reduce the likelihood of equipment failure on the water.

Finally, understanding the specific techniques associated with your rod and reel can significantly improve your effectiveness in targeting largemouth bass. Techniques such as flipping, pitching, and casting can all be influenced by the gear you use. Practice these techniques to develop your skills and gain a better understanding of how your rod and reel interact with different lures. By mastering the mechanics of your fishing gear, you will be well-equipped to tackle the challenges of catching largemouth bass in lakes, ultimately increasing your chances of a successful outing.

Fishing Line Types and Strengths

When it comes to fishing for largemouth bass in lakes, understanding the various types of fishing lines and their strengths is crucial for success. The main types of fishing lines used are monofilament, fluorocarbon, and braid, each offering unique benefits and drawbacks. Monofilament line is a popular choice due to its elasticity, which provides excellent shock absorption. This feature is particularly beneficial when fishing in heavy cover, as it allows for better control during fights and reduces the chances of breaking the line. Additionally, monofilament is often more affordable and easier to handle, making it a good option for beginners.

Fluorocarbon line is another excellent choice for targeting largemouth bass, particularly in clear water conditions. One of its standout features is its low visibility underwater, which can be a significant advantage when bass are wary of fishing lines. Furthermore, fluorocarbon is denser than monofilament, allowing it to sink faster, making it suitable for deeper fishing applications.

Its abrasion resistance is also noteworthy, which is beneficial when fishing around rocks or other potential snags. However, fluorocarbon can be more rigid and less forgiving than monofilament, which may require anglers to adjust their techniques accordingly.

Braid is a third option that is gaining popularity among bass anglers for its strength and sensitivity. Braid is made from woven fibers, resulting in a thinner diameter compared to monofilament and fluorocarbon at the same strength rating. This thinness allows anglers to spool more line on their reels, providing longer casts and improved control over lures.

Additionally, braid has minimal stretch, which enhances sensitivity and allows anglers to feel even the slightest bites. However, the lack of stretch could be a disadvantage when using techniques that require a softer hook set, as it may lead to pulled hooks in certain situations.

When selecting a fishing line for largemouth bass, strength is a key consideration. The pound-test rating of a line indicates its breaking strength, and choosing the appropriate strength is essential based on your fishing environment and techniques. For instance, fishing in heavy cover or around thick vegetation typically calls for a stronger line, often rated between 30 to 65 pounds for braid. Conversely, lighter lines, between 10 to 20 pounds, may be more suitable for open water scenarios or when using finesse techniques. Understanding the relationship between line type and strength allows anglers to make informed choices that enhance their fishing experience.

Ultimately, the choice of fishing line will depend on personal preferences, fishing conditions, and the specific techniques being employed. Each type of line offers distinct advantages that can be leveraged to improve chances of success. By experimenting with different lines and understanding their characteristics, anglers can tailor their setups to better target largemouth bass. Whether you opt for monofilament, fluorocarbon, or braid, being well-informed about the strengths and weaknesses of each line type will contribute to your effectiveness on the water.

Tackle Boxes and Accessories

Tackle boxes and accessories are essential components for any successful largemouth bass fishing expedition. A well-organized tackle box not only saves time but also enhances your efficiency on the water. When selecting a tackle box, consider the size and layout that best suits your fishing style. Options range from soft-sided bags to hard-shell boxes, each offering varying levels of portability and organization. Look for a model with adjustable compartments that can accommodate various lures, hooks, and terminal tackle, allowing you to customize the storage according to your needs.

When it comes to accessories, a diverse selection of lures is crucial for attracting largemouth bass. Common types include crankbaits, spinnerbaits, jigs, and soft plastics. Each type of lure serves a specific purpose and can be used effectively in different conditions. For example, crankbaits are ideal for covering large areas quickly, while jigs can be targeted around structures where bass often hide.

Ensure your tackle box contains a variety of sizes, colors, and styles to match the local forage and water conditions.

In addition to lures, terminal tackle such as hooks, weights, and leader lines should not be overlooked. A quality selection of hooks in various sizes is vital for rigging your lures correctly and ensuring effective hook sets. Weights come in many forms, including bullet weights and split shots, and are essential for managing your lure's depth and presentation. Lastly, incorporating a variety of leader lines, such as fluorocarbon or braided line, allows you to adapt to different fishing environments and enhances your chances of landing a trophy bass.

Organizing your tackle box goes beyond just the lures and terminal tackle; including tools and accessories can greatly improve your fishing experience. Items such as pliers, scissors, and a fishing knife are indispensable for handling lures and making quick adjustments. A fish gripper or net is also essential for safely landing larger bass without causing harm to the fish.

Additionally, consider adding a small first aid kit and sunscreen to your tackle box to ensure you're prepared for a long day on the water.

Lastly, keeping your tackle box well-maintained is key to longevity and effectiveness. Regularly check for rust on hooks and corrosion on other metal components, replacing any damaged items promptly. Clean your lures to remove dirt and debris, which can affect their performance. An organized and well-maintained tackle box not only enhances your fishing efficiency but also provides peace of mind, allowing you to focus on what matters most: the thrill of catching largemouth bass.

Baits and Lures

Baits and lures play a critical role in successful largemouth bass fishing, as they mimic the natural prey that bass are accustomed to hunting. Understanding the differences between live baits and artificial lures is essential for any angler looking to improve their catch rate.

Live baits, such as minnows, worms, and crayfish, are often preferred because they provide a scent and movement that bass find irresistible. When using live bait, it is important to match the size and type of bait to the local forage in the lake. For example, if shad are prevalent in the water, using a live minnow can increase your chances of attracting larger bass.

Artificial lures come in a variety of shapes, sizes, and colors, each designed to imitate specific types of prey. Common categories of lures include crankbaits, spinnerbaits, buzzbaits, and soft plastics. Crankbaits are effective for covering large areas of water quickly, as they can be retrieved at various depths, while spinnerbaits are excellent for fishing in cover due to their weedless design.

Buzzbaits create surface commotion that can trigger aggressive strikes, particularly during low-light conditions. Soft plastics, such as worms and creature baits, are versatile and can be rigged in multiple ways, allowing anglers to adapt to different fishing scenarios.

Color selection is another vital aspect of choosing the right lure. Bass can be particularly sensitive to color, especially in clear water where visibility is high. Natural colors like green pumpkin, watermelon, or shad patterns tend to work well in clear conditions, while brighter colors, such as chartreuse or fire tiger, can be effective in murky waters. It is advisable to carry a range of colors in your tackle box and to experiment until you find what works best for the specific lake conditions you are facing.

The presentation of baits and lures is equally important as the choice of bait itself. Varying the speed and technique used to retrieve your lure can make a significant difference in attracting bass. For instance, a slow and steady retrieve may work well for crankbaits, while a stop-and-go technique can be effective for spinnerbaits and soft plastics. Additionally, incorporating pauses or erratic movements can simulate the behavior of injured prey, enticing bass to strike. Understanding the behavior of bass in relation to water temperature, time of day, and weather conditions will help you fine-tune your presentation for optimal results.

Finally, successful bass fishing often requires a combination of patience and adaptability. Observing the environment and being willing to change your approach based on the bass's response to your baits and lures is crucial. Whether you are on a fishing trip or a leisurely day on the lake, experimenting with different baits, colors, and techniques can lead to improved success rates. By mastering the art of choosing and presenting baits and lures effectively, you will enhance your ability to catch largemouth bass and enjoy the rewarding experience that comes with it.

Chapter 3

Choosing the Right Location

Best Lakes for Largemouth Bass

When targeting largemouth bass, choosing the right lake is crucial to your success. Several lakes across the United States are renowned for their thriving populations of largemouth bass. These lakes not only offer ample fishing opportunities but also feature diverse habitats that support healthy bass growth.

Some of the best lakes for largemouth bass fishing include Lake Guntersville in Alabama, Clear Lake in California, and Lake Okeechobee in Florida. Each of these locations presents unique conditions that cater to both novice and experienced anglers looking to catch trophy-sized bass.

Lake Guntersville, Alabama, is often hailed as one of the premier bass fishing destinations in the country. Spanning over 69,000 acres, this expansive lake features a variety of habitats, including grass beds, submerged timber, and shallow flats. The abundant vegetation provides excellent cover for largemouth bass, making it an ideal environment for both spawning and feeding.

Anglers frequently report success using a range of techniques, such as flipping jigs in heavy cover or casting topwater lures during early mornings and late evenings. The lake's consistent bass population and the potential for catching fish exceeding ten pounds make it a must-visit for any serious bass fisherman.

Clear Lake in California is another exceptional destination for largemouth bass fishing. Known for its clear waters and abundant forage, this lake covers approximately 43,000 acres and is recognized for producing large fish. The unique geography of Clear Lake, with its rocky shorelines and submerged islands, creates numerous hotspots where bass can be found.

Techniques such as crankbait fishing along the rocky banks or using soft plastics in the lake's many coves can lead to impressive catches. Moreover, the lake's warming temperatures throughout the spring months trigger aggressive feeding behavior in bass, making it an ideal time for anglers to visit.

Lake Okeechobee in Florida stands out as one of the largest freshwater lakes in the United States and is well-known for its exceptional largemouth bass fishing. Covering over 730 square miles, Okeechobee features expansive marshes, lily pads, and submerged grass beds that serve as prime habitats for bass. The lake's nutrient-rich waters support a thriving ecosystem, attracting both baitfish and larger predators.

Anglers can benefit from techniques such as flipping and pitching into heavy cover or using spinnerbaits in open water. The lake's warm climate allows for year-round fishing, making it a favorite among anglers seeking consistent action throughout the seasons.

Finally, Lake Champlain, straddling the border between New York and Vermont, offers another excellent opportunity for largemouth bass fishing. This lake is known for its diverse habitats, ranging from rocky shores to expansive weed beds, which attract a variety of fish species. The combination of deep and shallow areas provides anglers with a range of fishing styles, from deep-water jigging to surface fishing in the shallows.

Seasonal patterns also play a significant role in fishing success here, with spring and fall being particularly productive times to target largemouth bass. As one of the largest lakes in the northeastern United States, Lake Champlain continuously produces impressive catches, making it a sought-after destination for bass anglers.

Understanding Lake Ecosystems

Lake ecosystems are complex environments that support a diverse range of flora and fauna, each playing a crucial role in maintaining the balance of the ecosystem. Understanding the intricacies of ecosystems is essential for anglers interested in fishing for largemouth bass.

Lakes are typically divided into three distinct zones: the littoral zone, the limnetic zone, and the benthic zone. Each zone offers different habitats and resources, influencing where largemouth bass are likely to be found at various times.

The littoral zone, located near the shore, is characterized by shallow waters, abundant sunlight, and significant vegetation. This area is vital for the spawning of largemouth bass as it provides shelter and food sources such as insects, smaller fish, and crustaceans.

The presence of aquatic plants not only offers hiding spots for bass but also attracts other species that serve as prey. Understanding the dynamics of this zone can greatly enhance an angler's chances of locating bass, especially during the spring and summer months when they are more active.

Moving away from the shore, the limnetic zone represents the open water area of the lake, where light penetrates and supports a different set of life forms. This zone is often rich in plankton and smaller fish, which are essential food sources for largemouth bass. During warmer months, bass may venture into this zone to feed, particularly during low-light conditions such as dawn and dusk. Anglers should consider using techniques like trolling or casting with swimbaits in the limnetic zone to effectively target bass that are actively hunting for prey.

The benthic zone, located at the bottom of the lake, is often overlooked but plays a significant role in the overall ecosystem. This area is home to decomposers and detritivores that break down organic matter, contributing to nutrient cycling within the lake. Largemouth bass often forage in this zone, particularly during the warmer months when they seek out prey hiding among rocks, logs, and other structures. Understanding the bottom composition of the lake and utilizing techniques such as jigging or dragging soft plastics can help anglers successfully target bass that are feeding close to the lakebed.

In addition to these zones, factors such as water temperature, clarity, and seasonal changes also influence the behavior of largemouth bass within lake ecosystems. Anglers must adapt their techniques and strategies according to these variables to maximize their success. By gaining a deeper understanding of lake ecosystems, including the interactions between different species and the importance of habitat structure, anglers can make informed decisions that will enhance their fishing experience and increase their chances of landing that trophy largemouth bass.

Seasonal Patterns and Their Impact

Understanding seasonal patterns is crucial for effectively fishing largemouth bass in lakes. These patterns dictate the behavior and location of bass throughout the year, influenced by factors such as water temperature, forage availability, and spawning cycles. Each season presents distinct opportunities and challenges that anglers must recognize to enhance their chances of success.

In spring, as water temperatures begin to rise, largemouth bass become increasingly active after the lethargy of winter. This season marks the onset of the spawning period, usually occurring when water temperatures reach 60 to 75 degrees Fahrenheit (16°C to 24°C). During this time, males establish nests in shallow areas, making them more aggressive and territorial. Anglers can capitalize on this behavior by utilizing topwater lures and shallow-running baits, particularly in areas near vegetation or structure where bass tend to spawn.

Summer brings warmer temperatures and often leads to a decline in bass activity during the hottest parts of the day. During this season, bass typically seek cooler waters, often found in deeper areas or near submerged structures. Anglers should adjust their tactics accordingly, using techniques such as drop-shotting or Carolina rigging to target bass in deeper water. Additionally, early morning and late evening are prime times for fishing when temperatures are more favorable, and bass are more likely to be feeding near the surface.

As fall approaches, water temperatures begin to drop, signaling a shift in bass behavior once again. This season is marked by increased feeding activity as bass prepare for winter. They become more mobile and often chase schools of baitfish in shallower waters. Anglers should focus on using reaction baits like crankbaits and spinnerbaits, which can effectively mimic the erratic movements of prey. Additionally, targeting areas where baitfish congregate will significantly increase the chances of catching larger bass.

Winter presents the most challenging conditions for bass fishing, as these fish become less active due to cold water temperatures. During this season, they retreat to deeper waters and become more lethargic, making them less likely to chase after fast-moving lures. Successful winter fishing requires patience and the use of finesse techniques such as jigging or slow presentations with soft plastics. Understanding these seasonal patterns allows anglers to adapt their approaches, ensuring a more rewarding fishing experience throughout the year.

Chapter 4

Techniques for Catching Largemouth Bass

Casting Techniques

Casting techniques are crucial for successfully targeting largemouth bass in lakes, as the right method can significantly increase your chances of a productive fishing trip. Understanding the various casting techniques allows anglers to present lures and baits in ways that mimic the natural movements of prey, which is essential for enticing bass.

This subchapter will explore several effective casting techniques that every angler should master to enhance their fishing experience.

The overhead cast is one of the most fundamental techniques in bass fishing. This method involves raising the rod above your head and casting forward in a smooth motion. To perform an effective overhead cast, anglers should grip the rod firmly and use their wrist to flick the rod tip forward as they release the line. This technique allows for long distances and can cover larger areas of water, making it ideal for open lakes. Additionally, mastering the overhead cast enables anglers to reach distant structures or vegetation where bass may be hiding.

Another important technique is the sidearm cast, which is especially useful in situations where accuracy is critical. This casting style involves keeping the rod parallel to the water's surface and swinging it to the side. The sidearm cast is effective for avoiding obstacles such as overhanging branches or when fishing in tighter spaces. By using the sidearm technique, anglers can deliver lures with precision, allowing them to target specific spots where bass are likely to be lurking. Practicing this technique can greatly improve an angler's ability to land lures in the desired location.

The pitch cast is a specialized technique that allows anglers to make short, accurate casts with minimal splash. This method is particularly effective when fishing in heavy cover, such as lily pads or submerged vegetation, where bass often seek shelter. To execute a pitch cast, the angler holds the rod at a 45-degree angle and uses a quick flick of the wrist to propel the lure forward while keeping the line taut. This technique not only reduces disturbance in the water but also presents the lure in a natural manner that bass find enticing. Becoming proficient in pitch casting can significantly enhance an angler's success in dense cover.

Finally, the roll cast is an essential technique for anglers who find themselves in areas where a traditional overhead cast may not be feasible. This method allows for casting in tight spaces and is particularly useful in flowing water or around obstacles. To perform a roll cast, the angler begins with the rod tip low and swings it back before flicking it forward, allowing the line to roll off the rod tip.

This technique provides a smooth presentation and can be particularly effective when targeting bass in streams or along the edges of lakes. By mastering the roll cast, anglers can expand their fishing opportunities in various environments.

In conclusion, mastering various casting techniques is vital for successfully fishing for largemouth bass in lakes. Each technique—overhead, sidearm, pitch, and roll—serves specific purposes and is suited for different fishing scenarios. By practicing these casting methods and understanding when to utilize each one, anglers can significantly improve their chances of catching largemouth bass and enhance their overall fishing experience. Investing time in honing these skills will pay off during those critical moments on the water.

Trolling Techniques

Trolling for largemouth bass can be an effective technique, particularly in larger lakes where fish are dispersed.

This method involves pulling baits through the water at a controlled speed, allowing anglers to cover significant areas and locate active fish. One of the primary advantages of trolling is that it enables the use of multiple lines simultaneously, increasing the chances of hooking a fish. Furthermore, it allows for the exploration of various depths by adjusting the trolling speed and the type of lure used.

When selecting lures for trolling, it is essential to consider the size and color that mimic the natural forage of largemouth bass in the specific lake. Crankbaits are a popular choice due to their ability to create a realistic swimming action. Deep-diving crankbaits can be particularly effective when targeting bass in deeper water, while shallow-running models work well in the upper layers.

Additionally, spinnerbaits and swimbaits can be effective, especially when bass are feeding aggressively. Matching the lure color to the water clarity and the prevailing weather conditions can also enhance success.

Speed is a crucial factor in trolling. Generally, a speed of 2 to 4 miles per hour works well, but it can vary based on the activity level of the fish. Slower speeds may be more effective during colder months or when the fish are less active, while faster speeds can provoke strikes during warmer months when bass are more aggressive. Experimenting with different speeds can help determine the optimal pace for the conditions on a given day.

Another important aspect of trolling is the positioning of the boat. Maintaining a consistent trolling path is vital to ensure that the lures swim effectively and remain in the strike zone. Anglers should consider using a GPS to mark productive areas and keep track of their routes.

It is also beneficial to troll in areas where structure, such as submerged vegetation, fallen trees, or rocky outcrops, is present, as these are known habitats for largemouth bass. Adjusting the trolling path to circle back through these hotspots can lead to increased catch rates.

Finally, monitoring the equipment is essential to successful trolling. Using a quality rod and reel combo, along with appropriate line strength, can make a significant difference when battling a large bass. Additionally, using planer boards can help spread lines further apart, allowing for more effective coverage of the water column. Regularly checking for weeds or debris on the lures will ensure they remain effective. With practice and attention to detail, trolling can become a productive method for catching largemouth bass in lakes, enhancing the overall fishing experience.

Fly Fishing for Largemouth Bass

Fly fishing for largemouth bass offers an exhilarating challenge that combines both skill and strategy. While traditionally associated with species like trout and salmon, fly fishing can be an effective method for targeting bass, particularly in lakes where these fish thrive. The key to success lies in understanding the unique behavior of largemouth bass and the specific techniques that cater to their feeding habits.

By employing the right gear, selecting suitable flies, and mastering casting techniques, anglers can significantly increase their chances of landing these prized fish.

Choosing the right gear is essential when fly fishing for largemouth bass. A medium to heavy fly rod, typically ranging from 8 to 10 weight, is recommended to handle the size and strength of bass. This rod should be paired with a matching fly reel that has a smooth drag system to manage the powerful runs of a hooked bass. A weight-forward floating line is generally the best choice, allowing for easier casting and better control over the fly's presentation.

Additionally, using a tapered leader with a heavier tippet can withstand the abrasive environments that bass often inhabit, such as submerged logs and rocky structures.

Selecting the appropriate flies is crucial for enticing largemouth bass. Streamers are highly effective, mimicking the movement of baitfish, which are a primary food source for bass. Patterns such as Clouser minnows or deceivers can be particularly successful.

Additionally, poppers and surface flies can create exciting surface action during warmer months when bass are actively feeding near the surface. Color selection can vary depending on water clarity and weather conditions; brighter colors often work well in murky waters, while more natural colors can be effective in clear conditions. Experimenting with different patterns and sizes can help anglers find what triggers a strike on a given day.

Casting techniques tailored for bass fishing can greatly enhance effectiveness. Accuracy and distance are important, particularly when targeting bass hiding near cover such as weed beds, docks, or fallen trees. Roll casts and sidearm casts allow for better presentations in tight situations.

Moreover, learning to double-haul can increase line speed and distance, making it easier to reach distant targets. Once the fly lands, incorporating a variety of retrieves, such as stripping, twitching, or pausing, can mimic the action of injured prey and entice bass to strike.

Understanding the behavior and feeding patterns of largemouth bass is essential for successful fly fishing. Bass tend to be most active during dawn and dusk, making these times prime for fishing. During warmer months, they often move to shallow waters to feed, while in cooler months, they may retreat to deeper structures. Observing water temperature, weather conditions, and the presence of baitfish can help anglers pinpoint the best times and locations to fish.

Additionally, recognizing the bass's mood—whether they are aggressive or more cautious—can guide the angler in selecting the right approach and technique.

Fly fishing for largemouth bass not only requires specialized techniques but also an understanding of the environment and fish behavior. By equipping themselves with the right gear, selecting appropriate flies, mastering casting techniques, and being mindful of the bass's feeding patterns, anglers can enjoy a rewarding experience on the water. As the popularity of fly fishing continues to grow, it opens up new avenues for exploring the dynamic world of bass fishing, allowing enthusiasts to connect with nature while pursuing their passion for the sport.

How To Fish For Largemouth Bass In Lakes

A Practical Guide to Techniques, Tactics, and Gear

Chapter 5

Tactics for Success

Time of Day Considerations

Understanding the time of day is crucial for successfully fishing largemouth bass in lakes. Bass are known to exhibit different behaviors and feeding patterns depending on the light conditions. Early morning and late afternoon are often considered prime times for bass fishing. During these hours, the low light levels encourage bass to venture into shallower waters in search of prey.

As the sun rises higher in the sky, bass tend to seek shelter in deeper waters or around structures, making them less accessible to anglers. Recognizing these patterns can help you plan your fishing trips to align with the most active feeding times of the day.

Midday typically presents a challenge for anglers targeting largemouth bass. As the sun reaches its peak, the water temperature rises, prompting bass to retreat to cooler depths or shaded areas. During this time, bass are less likely to chase after bait, which can make fishing more difficult. However, this period can be utilized by employing specific tactics, such as targeting shaded spots created by overhanging trees, docks, or submerged structures. Additionally, using finesse techniques and lighter tackle can entice more wary bass that may be resting during the heat of the day.

As evening approaches, the conditions shift again, often leading to another productive fishing window. The setting sun creates a transition period where bass become more active, feeding in preparation for the night. This time is particularly effective for surface lures, as bass may rise to take advantage of insects and smaller fish that become more active at dusk. Anglers should focus on areas where the water meets the shore, as this is where bass will likely be hunting. The evening is also an excellent time to experiment with different types of lures and presentations, as bass can be more aggressive and willing to strike.

Night fishing for largemouth bass can offer unique advantages. Under the cover of darkness, bass often venture into shallower waters to hunt, making them more accessible to anglers. The use of dark-colored lures or those that create noise can be particularly effective during nighttime fishing. Additionally, utilizing a good light source can help in attracting both the bass and their prey, as many smaller fish and insects are drawn to light. It is essential to remain aware of your surroundings during night fishing, as navigating lakes can present challenges when visibility is low.

In summary, understanding the time of day and its impact on largemouth bass behavior is vital for successful fishing. By recognizing the patterns associated with morning, midday, evening, and night, anglers can adapt their tactics and gear to maximize their chances of landing a catch. Keeping a fishing journal to note the times and conditions that yield the best results can further enhance your fishing strategy. With patience and practice, anglers can leverage these insights to improve their overall fishing experience and success on the water.

Weather Conditions and Their Effects

Weather conditions play a critical role in the behavior and patterns of largemouth bass in lakes. Understanding how various weather elements impact fishing can significantly enhance your chances of success on the water. Factors such as temperature, cloud cover, wind, and precipitation can influence bass activity, feeding habits, and their overall location within a lake. By recognizing these patterns, anglers can adjust their tactics and gear to align with the conditions, ultimately maximizing their fishing experience.

Temperature is one of the most significant weather factors affecting largemouth bass. As ectothermic creatures, bass rely on their environment to regulate their body temperature. In warmer months, water temperatures above 70 degrees Fahrenheit typically signal increased activity, prompting bass to feed more aggressively. Conversely, during colder months, bass become lethargic and may retreat to deeper waters or cover.

Anglers should pay attention to the seasonal temperature changes and adjust their fishing times accordingly, focusing on early mornings or late afternoons during warmer weather when bass are most active.

Cloud cover can also influence bass behavior. On overcast days, the diffused light can encourage bass to roam more freely in shallow waters, making them easier to catch. The reduced visibility allows them to venture out from their hiding spots to hunt for prey. Conversely, bright sunny days often push bass into deeper, cooler water or shady areas, such as under docks or overhanging trees. Understanding these preferences can help anglers decide where to cast their lines based on the day's weather conditions.

Wind is another important element that can affect bass fishing. A light breeze can create ripples on the water's surface, which can help to mask an angler's presence and encourage bass to feed near the surface. Wind can also push baitfish towards the shore, attracting larger predators like largemouth bass.

However, strong winds can make fishing more challenging, as they create choppy water and complicate casting accuracy. On windy days, anglers should consider using heavier lures to maintain control and target areas where the wind creates current breaks, which often attract feeding bass.

Precipitation can have varied effects on fishing for largemouth bass. Rain can improve fishing conditions by oxygenating the water and increasing activity levels among bass. The aftermath of a rainstorm can also lead to runoff, which can bring nutrients and food sources into the water, making it an ideal time for fishing. However, heavy rains can cause water levels to rise rapidly, altering the lake's structure and potentially pushing bass into new areas. Anglers should remain adaptable and prepared to shift their strategies based on how recent rainfall has impacted the lake's environment and the behavior of the fish.

Chapter 6

Catch and Release Practices

Importance of Conservation

Conservation plays a crucial role in sustaining the ecosystems that support largemouth bass populations. Healthy lakes are not only essential for the fish but also for the overall biodiversity that thrives in these environments.

As anglers, understanding the importance of conservation helps ensure that future generations can enjoy fishing experiences similar to those we have today. By preserving the habitats and water quality, we contribute to the longevity of the species and the enjoyment of the sport.

One of the key aspects of bass conservation is maintaining the balance within the aquatic ecosystem. Largemouth bass are both predators and prey, and their populations can significantly impact the populations of other species in the lake. Overfishing, pollution, and habitat destruction can disrupt this balance, leading to declines in fish health and numbers. By practicing responsible fishing techniques, such as catch and release, anglers can help mitigate these effects and promote a sustainable environment for all aquatic life.

Water quality is another critical factor in the conservation of largemouth bass. Pollutants, such as fertilizers, pesticides, and waste runoff, can lead to harmful algal blooms and other issues that degrade water quality. These problems can directly affect bass health and reproductive success. Anglers can contribute to conservation efforts by advocating for clean water initiatives, participating in lake clean-up events, and being mindful of their own impact on the environment when fishing.

Habitat preservation is equally important in the conservation of largemouth bass. Natural structures such as submerged vegetation, fallen trees, and rocks provide essential cover and breeding grounds for bass. Unfortunately, human activities, such as shoreline development and dredging, can destroy these habitats. Anglers can support conservation by promoting responsible land use practices and participating in local conservation programs that aim to restore and protect these vital habitats.

Finally, education and awareness about conservation are vital for fostering a community dedicated to protecting our natural resources. By sharing knowledge about sustainable fishing practices and the importance of preserving aquatic ecosystems, anglers can inspire others to take action. Joining local fishing clubs or conservation organizations can amplify these efforts, creating a collective voice for the protection of our lakes and the species that inhabit them. Emphasizing conservation helps ensure that the thrill of fishing for largemouth bass continues for years to come.

Best Practices for Catch and Release

When practicing catch and release, the foremost goal is to ensure the fish has the best chance of survival after being caught. This begins with proper handling techniques. When lifting a largemouth bass out of the water, it is crucial to keep the fish in a horizontal position to prevent damage to its internal organs. Use both hands, with one supporting the belly and the other firm on the tail. Avoid using a net with large holes, as this can cause unnecessary stress and injury to the fish. Additionally, wetting your hands before touching the bass will help protect its slime coating, which is vital for its health.

Timing is another essential aspect of successful catch and release practices. Avoid fishing during the hottest parts of the day when water temperatures are elevated, as this can stress the fish more significantly. Early morning or late evening are ideal times to target largemouth bass, allowing them to be caught while the water is cooler.

If you must fish during the heat, minimize the time the fish spends out of the water and be prepared to release it quickly. The quicker the release, the better the chances for recovery.

Using the right tackle and bait can also play a critical role in catch and release success. Select hooks designed to minimize injury, such as circle hooks, which tend to hook fish in the corner of the mouth rather than deep in the throat. Additionally, consider using barbless hooks or crimping down the barbs on your hooks, making it easier to release the fish without causing excessive harm. This approach not only benefits the fish but can also enhance your fishing experience by making releases smoother and quicker.

When it comes to photographing your catch, it's important to prioritize the fish's welfare. Minimize the time the fish is out of water and avoid holding it vertically, which can place strain on its body. Instead, keep the fish close to the water's surface for photos and support its weight properly.

If possible, use a landing mat or a soft surface to minimize the impact on the fish when handling it for pictures. After capturing that perfect shot, return the fish back to the water gently, allowing it to regain its strength before swimming away.

Finally, it is crucial to educate fellow anglers about the importance of catch and release. Sharing best practices not only contributes to the sustainability of largemouth bass populations but also fosters a sense of community among anglers.

Encourage others to follow the same respectful practices, emphasizing the long-term benefits of maintaining healthy fish populations for future generations. By collectively adopting responsible fishing habits, anglers can enjoy the sport while ensuring the well-being of the species they cherish.

Handling Largemouth Bass Safely

Handling largemouth bass safely is crucial for both the angler and the fish. When fishing for these popular species, it is important to minimize stress and injury to the fish to ensure their survival after being released. Largemouth bass are resilient, but improper handling can lead to damage to their sensitive skin and fins, as well as harm their internal organs. Understanding the proper techniques for handling these fish will not only promote ethical fishing practices but also enhance the overall fishing experience.

Before you even catch a largemouth bass, it is essential to prepare your gear and approach. Use a landing net with a soft, nylon mesh to minimize injury when bringing the fish on board. Avoid using nets with rubberized or abrasive materials, as these can harm the fish's slime coat, a protective layer essential for their health. When you have a fish on the line, keep your rod tip up to tire the fish out gradually, avoiding sudden jerks or pulls that could injure it. Once the fish is close enough to net, be gentle and swift in your actions.

Once you have landed a largemouth bass, it is crucial to handle it with care. Wet your hands before touching the fish to protect its slime coat, which helps prevent infections. Always support the fish horizontally by placing one hand under its belly and the other around the tail. This method ensures that the fish does not experience undue stress or injury. Avoid holding the fish vertically by its jaw, as this can cause severe damage to its internal organs and jaw structure, especially if the fish is large.

If you plan to release the bass, minimize the time it spends out of the water. Use a quick photograph method if you want to document your catch, ensuring that the fish is in a stable position and your hands are wet. When it comes to releasing the fish, gently place it back into the water headfirst, allowing it to regain its bearings. If the fish appears lethargic, hold it upright in the water to help circulate water over its gills until it swims away on its own. This practice significantly increases the chances of survival after release.

Educating fellow anglers and promoting safe handling practices is equally important. Encourage others to follow the same techniques to protect the largemouth bass population and the ecosystem as a whole. Share your knowledge on social media, fishing forums, or local fishing clubs to raise awareness about the significance of proper fish handling. By fostering a culture of respect for these fish, anglers can contribute to sustainable fishing practices that benefit future generations.

Chapter 7

Common Mistakes to Avoid

Overlooking Environmental Factors

When fishing for largemouth bass, overlooking environmental factors can significantly impact your success. These factors include water temperature, clarity, and structure, all of which play crucial roles in determining the behavior and feeding patterns of bass. Understanding how each of these elements interacts with the ecosystem can enhance your fishing strategy and increase your chances of landing a trophy-sized bass.

Water temperature is one of the most critical environmental factors to consider. Largemouth bass are cold-blooded creatures, meaning their body temperature is regulated by the surrounding water.

During warmer months, bass are generally more active and can be found in shallower waters, particularly in the early morning and late evening.

Conversely, as temperatures drop in the fall or during colder months, bass seek deeper, more stable waters. Being aware of seasonal temperature changes can help you choose the best times to fish and the appropriate depths to target.

Water clarity is another essential factor that can influence bass behavior. Clear water allows for greater visibility, which can lead bass to become more cautious and harder to catch. In such conditions, using more natural colors and subtle presentations can be effective. In contrast, murky or stained water can encourage bass to feed more aggressively, allowing for bolder lures and brighter colors to attract their attention. Assessing water clarity before you start fishing can guide your lure selection and presentation techniques.

The structure of the lake also plays a vital role in the habitat preferences of largemouth bass. They tend to thrive around structures such as submerged trees, rocks, grass beds, and docks, which provide cover and ambush points for hunting prey. When fishing, focus on these areas as they can significantly increase your chances of encountering bass. Utilizing techniques like flipping or pitching can help you effectively present your bait in these complex environments.

Lastly, weather conditions can further complicate the equation. Changes in barometric pressure, wind, and precipitation can all influence fish behavior. For instance, bass may become more active during overcast days or just before a storm. On sunny days, they may seek shade beneath structures. Understanding how these environmental factors affect bass behavior can lead to more strategic fishing trips, allowing you to adapt your approach based on the conditions you encounter. By considering these environmental elements, you can enhance your overall fishing experience and improve your success in targeting largemouth bass.

Inappropriate Gear Choices

Inappropriate gear choices can significantly impact your success when fishing for largemouth bass in lakes. Understanding the right equipment is crucial, as using the wrong gear not only affects your ability to catch fish but can also lead to frustration and wasted time on the water. Selecting the appropriate rod, reel, line, and tackle is essential for maximizing your chances of landing quality bass.

One common mistake anglers make is using a fishing rod that is either too heavy or too light for the task at hand. A rod that is too heavy can lead to a lack of sensitivity, making it difficult to detect subtle bites. Conversely, a rod that is too light may not provide the necessary power to control larger fish. Ideally, for targeting largemouth bass, a medium to medium-heavy rod with a fast action tip is recommended. This setup provides the balance needed for casting, sensitivity, and power.

Equally important is the choice of reel. Many anglers opt for spinning reels due to their versatility, but baitcasting reels are often preferred for bass fishing because they offer better control and accuracy for casting heavy lures. Using a spinning reel with a heavier line than it can handle might lead to line twists and tangles, ultimately ruining your fishing experience. Selecting a gear ratio that allows for quick retrieval is also beneficial when bass are actively feeding.

The line you choose plays a pivotal role in your fishing success. Monofilament, fluorocarbon, and braided lines each have their advantages and disadvantages. Monofilament is forgiving and easy to handle, but may not provide the sensitivity needed for finesse techniques. Fluorocarbon is nearly invisible underwater and offers excellent sensitivity, but may be less durable against abrasions. Braided line, while strong and durable, can be more visible in clear water, making it crucial to consider the fishing conditions when selecting your line.

Lastly, tackle selection can make or break your fishing trip. Using lures that are not suited for the season or water conditions can result in poor performance. For example, using topwater lures during cold water periods or deep-diving crankbaits in shallow areas can lead to missed opportunities. It's important to match your tackle to the specific conditions of the lake you are fishing, including water temperature, structure, and the time of year, to ensure you are presenting the most effective offerings to the bass.

Ignoring Regulations

Ignoring regulations when fishing for largemouth bass can lead to serious consequences, both for the angler and the fish population. Regulations are put in place to ensure sustainable fishing practices and to protect the ecosystem. When anglers disregard these rules, they not only risk penalties but also contribute to the decline of bass populations, which can disrupt the entire aquatic community. Understanding and adhering to local laws is essential for maintaining healthy fisheries and ensuring future generations can enjoy the sport.

One common regulation that is often overlooked is the size and bag limits for largemouth bass. These limits are established based on extensive research and are designed to allow fish to reach maturity and reproduce before being harvested. Ignoring these limits can lead to overfishing, which diminishes the population and affects the overall health of the lake. Anglers should familiarize themselves with the specific regulations in their area, as these can vary widely from one location to another. Not only does respecting these limits support conservation efforts, but it also enhances the fishing experience by ensuring that there are ample fish available for future catches.

Another important aspect of fishing regulations involves the use of certain gear and techniques. Many states have restrictions on the types of baits, lures, and fishing methods that can be used for largemouth bass. For instance, the use of live bait may be prohibited in some areas to prevent the introduction of non-native species. Ignoring these gear regulations can lead to fines and potentially harm the local fish population.

Anglers should invest time in understanding the gear restrictions in their region and choosing appropriate equipment that aligns with the regulations, ensuring both compliance and the sustainability of the bass fishing experience.

Seasonal closures are another critical regulation that anglers must heed. Many jurisdictions implement closed seasons to allow fish to spawn without the added stress of fishing pressure. Overlooking these closures not only jeopardizes the spawning process but can also lead to significant legal repercussions. Anglers should stay informed about the seasonal regulations in their area, as fishing during a closed season can severely impact the future of largemouth bass populations. Following these guidelines helps to ensure that the fish can reproduce successfully, leading to healthier lakes and better fishing opportunities in the long run.

Ultimately, ignoring fishing regulations can have far-reaching consequences that extend beyond individual anglers. By adhering to these rules, fishermen contribute to the conservation of largemouth bass and the preservation of aquatic ecosystems. Responsible fishing practices not only enhance the quality of the fishing experience but also promote a culture of respect for nature. Anglers who prioritize compliance with regulations play a vital role in maintaining the integrity of lake environments, ensuring that future anglers can continue to enjoy the thrill of fishing for largemouth bass.

Chapter 8

Advanced Techniques and Strategies

Seasonal Adjustments in Strategy

Understanding seasonal adjustments in strategy is crucial for successfully targeting largemouth bass throughout the year. As water temperatures change, so do the behaviors and habits of bass. Each season presents unique conditions that affect where bass will be located, what they will be feeding on, and how anglers should present their baits.

By adapting your approach to align with seasonal patterns, you can significantly increase your chances of a productive fishing trip.

In spring, as water temperatures begin to rise, largemouth bass enter their spawning phase. This is typically when they move into shallower waters and become more aggressive, making them easier to locate. Anglers should focus on areas with structure, such as submerged rocks, vegetation, and shallow flats. Techniques such as flipping or pitching soft plastics and using topwater lures can be particularly effective. During this time, it's essential to be mindful of catch-and-release practices to protect spawning populations.

Summer brings warmer water temperatures and often leads to changes in bass behavior. As the heat intensifies, largemouth bass may retreat to deeper, cooler waters during the day. Early morning and late evening are prime times for fishing, as bass are more likely to venture into shallower areas to feed. Anglers should consider using deeper diving crankbaits or jigs and targeting shaded areas, such as those under docks or overhanging trees. Understanding the thermocline and where bass are likely to find their comfort zone can lead to more successful outings.

As fall approaches, the feeding frenzy begins as bass prepare for the winter months. This is an excellent time for anglers to target bass as they aggressively feed on baitfish that are also migrating. Look for areas where baitfish are abundant, and focus on the transition zones between shallow and deep water. Using swimbaits and crankbaits that mimic the local forage can yield great results. The cooling water temperatures also prompt bass to become more active during the day, allowing for more opportunities to catch them.

Winter presents the most significant challenge for anglers targeting largemouth bass. With cooler water temperatures, bass become less active and often seek out deeper waters. During this season, patience and technique are vital. Anglers should opt for slow presentations, using finesse techniques such as drop-shotting or using small jigs. Targeting deeper structures like ledges or underwater humps can prove beneficial. Additionally, ice fishing in areas where allowed can also provide opportunities to catch largemouth bass during the winter months. By understanding and adapting to these seasonal changes, anglers can enhance their fishing success year-round.

Understanding Fish Behavior

Understanding fish behavior is crucial for any angler looking to successfully catch largemouth bass. Largemouth bass are known for their aggressive feeding habits, but their behavior can be influenced by various factors, including water temperature, time of day, and seasonal changes. By observing and understanding these behaviors, anglers can significantly enhance their chances of catching more fish.

One key aspect of largemouth bass behavior is their feeding patterns. These fish are opportunistic feeders, often hunting in ambush-style. They prefer to stay close to cover, such as submerged vegetation, fallen trees, or rocky structures, where they can hide while waiting for prey. During warmer months, bass tend to be more active in the early morning and late evening, taking advantage of low light conditions to hunt. Understanding these feeding windows can help anglers plan their fishing trips to coincide with optimal times.

Seasonal changes also play a significant role in the behavior of largemouth bass. In the spring, as the water warms, bass move into shallower waters for spawning, making them more accessible to anglers. During this time, males are particularly aggressive in defending their nests, allowing for more opportunities to catch them. As summer approaches and the water temperature rises, bass may retreat to deeper, cooler waters, becoming less active and more challenging to catch. In fall, bass begin to feed heavily in preparation for winter, often returning to shallower areas, which can provide excellent fishing opportunities.

Another important factor influencing bass behavior is the presence of forage species. Largemouth bass primarily feed on smaller fish, crustaceans, and insects. The abundance and type of forage in a lake can dictate where bass will be found. For instance, if there is a significant population of shad or bluegill, bass will be more likely to congregate in those areas. Understanding the local ecosystem and identifying the main food sources can help anglers select the best fishing spots.

Lastly, weather conditions can impact bass behavior. Overcast days often lead to increased activity, as bass feel more secure in low light. Conversely, bright, sunny days can cause them to seek refuge in deeper water or under heavy cover. Wind can also affect their feeding patterns, with a light breeze often causing prey to become more active, thus attracting bass. By paying attention to these environmental factors, anglers can adapt their strategies to match the behavior of largemouth bass, ultimately increasing their success on the water.

Utilizing Technology in Bass Fishing

Utilizing technology in bass fishing has revolutionized the way anglers approach their craft, making it easier to locate and catch largemouth bass in lakes. Modern fishing technology includes a variety of tools and devices designed to enhance the fishing experience. One of the most significant advancements is the use of sonar and fish finders, which provide detailed underwater images and help identify the structure, depth, and presence of fish.

By using these devices, anglers can pinpoint the locations where bass are likely to be hiding, increasing their chances of a successful outing.

Another technological advancement is the use of GPS systems, which can be invaluable for bass fishing in larger lakes. GPS allows anglers to mark productive spots on the water, track their movements, and return to successful fishing locations with ease. This feature is especially beneficial for those who fish in expansive bodies of water where familiar landmarks may be few and far between. With GPS, anglers can create a personalized map of their favorite fishing areas, ensuring that they can replicate successful trips in the future.

In addition to fish finders and GPS, smartphone apps have become popular tools for bass fishing enthusiasts. These applications can provide weather forecasts, tide information, and even insights into recent fishing trends in specific lakes. Some apps allow anglers to log their catches, track conditions, and share experiences with fellow fishermen.

By utilizing these technologies, anglers can stay informed and adapt their strategies based on real-time data, ultimately improving their fishing success.

Drone technology is another exciting development in the realm of bass fishing. Drones can be used to scout fishing locations from above, helping anglers identify potential hotspots without disturbing the water. Moreover, drones equipped with cameras can provide a unique perspective on underwater structures and vegetation, giving fishermen a clearer understanding of the environment. This aerial view can be particularly helpful in spotting schools of fish or areas where bass may be congregating.

Finally, advancements in bait technology, such as electronic lures and smart fishing gear, are changing the way anglers attract and catch largemouth bass. Electronic lures can mimic the movements and sounds of prey, making them more enticing to fish. Furthermore, smart gear equipped with sensors can provide feedback on fishing conditions and even suggest optimal techniques based on current data.

By embracing these technological innovations, anglers can enhance their skills and increase their chances of landing trophy-sized largemouth bass in their favorite lakes.

Chapter 9

Local Regulations and Ethics

Fishing Licenses and Permits

Fishing licenses and permits are essential components of responsible fishing, particularly when targeting species like largemouth bass in lakes. Before embarking on any fishing trip, it is crucial to understand the legal requirements in your area.

Most states and countries mandate that anglers possess a valid fishing license, which helps regulate fish populations and maintain ecological balance. These licenses often vary in terms of duration, with options for daily, weekly, or annual permits, depending on how frequently you plan to fish.

When pursuing largemouth bass, it is important to check the specific regulations that apply to this species. Many jurisdictions implement size and bag limits to ensure sustainable fishing practices. These regulations can dictate the minimum length of fish that can be kept, as well as the maximum number of fish an angler can catch in a day. Familiarizing yourself with these rules not only helps protect the bass population but also enhances your fishing experience by ensuring compliance with local laws.

Acquiring a fishing license has become increasingly convenient with advancements in technology. Many states now offer online platforms where prospective anglers can easily purchase their licenses. In addition to online purchases, licenses can often be obtained at local bait shops, sporting goods stores, and government offices.

Be sure to have any required identification handy and to understand the payment methods accepted, as they can vary from one location to another.

In addition to fishing licenses, specific permits may be required for certain fishing methods or locations. For instance, if you plan to fish in a designated conservation area or utilize specialized techniques such as net fishing or ice fishing, additional permits may be necessary. It is advisable to research these requirements before your fishing trip to avoid any potential fines or legal issues. Consulting local wildlife agencies or online resources can provide clarity on the specific permits needed for your intended fishing activities.

Lastly, always remember to keep your fishing license and any relevant permits on hand while fishing. Many regions require anglers to display their licenses upon request from wildlife officials. Keeping your documentation organized and accessible not only ensures compliance with the law but also reflects a commitment to responsible fishing practices. By understanding and adhering to fishing license and permit regulations, you contribute to the conservation of largemouth bass and the overall health of aquatic ecosystems.

Understanding Size and Bag Limits

Understanding size and bag limits is crucial for anyone interested in fishing for largemouth bass in lakes. These regulations are established by wildlife agencies to promote sustainable fishing practices, protect fish populations, and ensure that future generations can enjoy the sport. Anglers must familiarize themselves with the specific guidelines for the body of water they are fishing, as these rules can vary widely from one location to another. The primary goal of these regulations is to maintain a healthy ecosystem and prevent overfishing, which can lead to declining fish populations and biodiversity loss.

Size limits refer to the minimum or maximum length of fish that can be legally kept. For largemouth bass, this often means that anglers may only keep fish that exceed a certain length, which is typically set to protect younger, breeding-sized fish. By allowing smaller fish to grow and reproduce, the regulations help sustain the population and promote a balanced age structure within the lake.

It is essential for anglers to measure their catch accurately using a proper measuring device, as violations can result in fines and a negative impact on local fish stocks.

Bag limits dictate the number of fish an angler can keep in a single day. This limit serves to prevent overharvesting and ensures that there are enough fish remaining in the ecosystem to support both the fishery and other anglers. For largemouth bass, bag limits may range from one to five fish, depending on the specific regulations of the lake or region. Understanding and adhering to these limits is not only a legal requirement but also a responsible practice that contributes to the health of the fishery.

In addition to size and bag limits, anglers should also be aware of seasonal regulations that may restrict fishing during certain times of the year. Many areas implement seasonal closures to protect spawning fish, allowing them to reproduce without the pressure of being harvested. These closures can vary based on geographic region and local fish populations.

Being aware of these seasonal restrictions is an essential part of responsible fishing practices, and it can also lead to better fishing experiences, as anglers can target fish during their optimal feeding and spawning times.

Finally, staying informed about changes to size and bag limits is vital for responsible fishing. Regulations can change based on scientific assessments of fish populations, environmental conditions, and public input. Anglers should regularly check with local wildlife agencies or consult their websites for updates.

By understanding and respecting size and bag limits, anglers contribute to the conservation of largemouth bass populations, ensuring that lakes remain vibrant and accessible for future generations of fishing enthusiasts.

Ethical Fishing Practices

Ethical fishing practices are essential for sustaining the delicate ecosystems that support largemouth bass populations in lakes. As anglers, it is our responsibility to ensure that our fishing activities do not harm the environment or the species we seek to catch. Understanding the principles of conservation, such as catch and release, responsible bait usage, and respecting fishing regulations, can help maintain healthy fish populations for future generations. Engaging in ethical fishing practices not only promotes the well-being of the fish but also enhances the overall fishing experience.

Catch and release is a fundamental practice that allows anglers to enjoy the thrill of fishing while minimizing the impact on fish populations. When practicing catch and release, it is crucial to handle the fish gently to reduce stress and injury. Use wet hands or a landing net to avoid removing the fish's protective slime coat, which is vital for its health.

Additionally, minimizing the time a fish spends out of water and using barbless hooks can significantly increase its chance of survival after being released. By adopting these practices, anglers can contribute to the sustainability of largemouth bass populations in their local lakes.

Responsible bait usage also plays a significant role in ethical fishing practices. When selecting bait, it is important to consider the potential impact on the ecosystem. Using live bait can introduce invasive species or disease, which may harm native fish populations.

Therefore, it is advisable to use artificial lures or locally sourced live bait that is permitted by local regulations. Moreover, understanding the feeding habits of largemouth bass can help anglers choose the most effective baits while minimizing ecological disruption.

Respecting fishing regulations is another crucial aspect of ethical fishing. Each region has specific rules regarding fishing seasons, size limits, and bag limits designed to protect fish populations and their habitats. Familiarizing oneself with these regulations not only ensures compliance but also helps in making informed decisions while fishing. By adhering to these guidelines, anglers can contribute to the conservation of largemouth bass and their habitats, fostering a healthier environment for all aquatic life.

Incorporating ethical fishing practices into your fishing routine not only benefits the environment but also enriches the experience of fishing itself. The satisfaction of knowing that you are contributing to the preservation of the species and the ecosystem elevates the sport beyond mere recreation. By promoting responsible fishing behaviors and encouraging fellow anglers to adopt these practices, we can collectively ensure that future generations of fishermen can enjoy the thrill of catching largemouth bass in thriving lakes.

Chapter 10

Conclusion and Next Steps

Recap of Key Points

In this section, we revisit the fundamental techniques and strategies that are crucial for successfully fishing for largemouth bass in lakes. Understanding the behavior and habitat preferences of largemouth bass is essential. These fish tend to thrive in warmer waters, often seeking shelter in structures such as submerged trees, rocks, and vegetation.

Recognizing the seasonal patterns and how they influence bass activity can significantly enhance your fishing experience. For instance, during the spawning season in spring, bass are more likely to be found in shallow waters, making them easier to target.

The choice of gear plays a pivotal role in your success on the water. Selecting the right rod, reel, and line can make a notable difference in your fishing efficiency. A medium to heavy action rod is typically recommended for largemouth bass, as it provides the strength needed to handle these powerful fish. Additionally, the reel should have a smooth drag system to manage sudden runs. The line type and strength should be chosen based on the cover you're fishing in; braided lines are often preferred for their durability and sensitivity, especially in heavy cover.

Lures and bait selection are crucial components of an effective fishing strategy. Various lures such as soft plastics, crankbaits, and topwater baits can be utilized depending on the conditions and time of day. Understanding how to match your lure to the prevailing water conditions and bass behavior can significantly improve your catch rate. For instance, using topwater lures during early morning or late evening can provoke aggressive strikes, while deeper diving crankbaits may be more effective during the heat of the day when bass retreat to cooler depths.

The importance of location and timing cannot be overstated. Successful bass anglers often emphasize the value of scouting and identifying productive spots before casting a line. Key areas such as points, coves, and creek channels should be prioritized, as they often serve as natural highways for bass. Furthermore, fishing at optimal times, such as dawn and dusk when bass are more actively feeding, can lead to a more fruitful outing. Combining strategic location choices with an understanding of bass behavior during different times of the day can enhance your chances of landing a trophy fish.

Lastly, maintaining a respectful and sustainable approach to fishing is vital. Practicing catch and release, adhering to local regulations, and being mindful of the environment are essential for preserving the fishing experience for future generations. By being aware of the impact of fishing on the ecosystem and taking steps to minimize it, anglers can contribute to the health of the fish populations. As you apply the techniques and strategies outlined in this guide, remember to enjoy the experience and foster a connection with nature while pursuing the exciting challenge of catching largemouth bass.

Resources for Further Learning

For those eager to deepen their understanding of fishing for largemouth bass, a variety of resources are available that cater to different learning preferences.

Books written by experts in the field provide in-depth knowledge on techniques, tactics, and gear. Titles such as "Largemouth Bass: The Complete Guide" and "In Pursuit of Giant Bass" offer valuable insights into the behavior of bass, seasonal patterns, and advanced fishing strategies. These texts often include illustrations and diagrams that can enhance the learning experience, making them beneficial for both novices and seasoned anglers.

Online platforms have revolutionized the way fishing enthusiasts access information. Websites dedicated to fishing, like BassResource and Fishbrain, offer articles, forums, and videos that focus on largemouth bass fishing. These platforms allow anglers to share their experiences, tips, and even local fishing reports.

Additionally, many experienced anglers maintain YouTube channels where they demonstrate fishing techniques, gear setups, and tackle reviews. Visual learners will find these resources particularly engaging as they can see the techniques in action.

Podcasts have emerged as another popular medium for learning about fishing. Various fishing podcasts host experts and experienced anglers who share their insights and stories related to largemouth bass fishing.

These auditory resources are ideal for those who prefer to learn on the go, whether commuting or enjoying a day outdoors. Listening to discussions about strategies, gear recommendations, and personal anecdotes can provide a deeper appreciation of the sport and inspire new approaches to fishing.

Attending workshops, seminars, or fishing expos can offer hands-on learning opportunities. Many organizations and local fishing clubs host events where anglers can learn from professionals in the field. These gatherings often include demonstrations of fishing techniques, discussions on seasonal patterns, and even opportunities to test new gear.

Engaging with fellow anglers in these settings can lead to valuable networking, allowing for the exchange of tips and experiences that can enhance one's fishing skills.

Finally, local libraries and community centers often provide access to fishing resources, including instructional videos and books. Many libraries also have fishing clubs that organize group outings, fostering a sense of community among local anglers. By utilizing these resources, aspiring largemouth bass fishers can gain knowledge, improve their skills, and ultimately enhance their fishing success in lakes.

Encouragement for the Journey Ahead

As you embark on your journey to master the art of fishing for largemouth bass, remember that every angler's experience is unique. The path you take will be shaped by your personal preferences, local conditions, and the resources available to you. Embrace the learning process, as it is filled with opportunities for growth and discovery.

Whether you are a novice or an experienced fisherman, the thrill of the catch lies not just in the size of the bass but in the moments spent on the water, the lessons learned, and the camaraderie often shared with fellow anglers.

One of the most important aspects of fishing is patience. Largemouth bass can be unpredictable, and there will be days when you find them elusive. Instead of becoming frustrated, view these moments as part of the journey. Use the time to reflect on your techniques, experiment with different lures, or simply enjoy the beauty of your surroundings.

Each outing is a chance to refine your skills, understand the behavior of the fish, and develop a deeper connection with nature. Celebrate the small victories, such as mastering a new casting technique or successfully identifying a promising fishing spot.

Networking with other anglers can significantly enhance your fishing journey. Engage with local fishing communities, whether through online forums, social media groups, or local fishing clubs. Sharing experiences, tips, and strategies can provide valuable insights that can help you improve.

You may discover new techniques or receive recommendations on gear that can enhance your fishing experience. Building relationships with fellow anglers fosters a sense of belonging and can lead to new fishing adventures, making the journey even more enjoyable.

Investing in quality gear is crucial for a successful fishing experience. While there are many options available, understanding what works best for you and the specific conditions you will face can make a significant difference. Research and seek advice on rods, reels, and lures that are effective for largemouth bass. However, remember that the most expensive gear does not guarantee success. Focus on becoming proficient with your equipment, as skill and knowledge often outweigh the advantages of high-end gear.

As you progress on your fishing journey, remember that it is not solely about the destination but the experiences along the way. Each trip will teach you something new, whether about fishing techniques, water conditions, or the very nature of largemouth bass themselves. Embrace the challenges, celebrate your achievements, and remain open to continuous learning. With every cast, you are not just fishing; you are building memories and honing your craft, ultimately enriching your life as an angler.

Author Notes & Acknowledgments

First and foremost, I would like to express my deepest gratitude to the people who inspired and supported me throughout the journey of writing this book. This project would not have been possible without their unwavering belief in me and their invaluable contributions.

To my wife, thank you for your constant encouragement and understanding. Your love and support have been my anchor during the challenging times of researching and writing this book. Your belief in my ability to make a difference in people's lives has been my driving force.

I would also like to disclose that this book contains some renewed artificial intelligence-generated content. I really appreciate very recent technological innovation by outstanding scientists and of course our reader's understanding.

Lastly, I want to express my deepest gratitude to the readers of this book. I sincerely hope the strategies and methods outlined within these pages will provide you with the knowledge and tools needed to truly make your life much better. Your commitment to seeking any good solutions and willingness to explore multiple methods is commendable.

Author Bio

Johnson is an amateur bass fisherman with an enthusiastic passion for the sport. He has gained extensive knowledge from professionals in the field and has accumulated significant experience in bass fishing. Over the years, Johnson has caught numerous largemouth bass, with the largest weighing over five pounds and measuring more than 52 centimeters in length.

Johnson Wu earned his MD in 1982. He has worked in hospitals in China & UK. Upon the recommendation of Sir Aaron Klug, the president of The Royal Society and a Nobel Prize winner in Chemistry, Dr. Wu was honorably awarded a British Royal Society Fellowship. He has published over 100 medical books and now practices medicine in Canada.

www.ingramcontent.com/pod-product-compliance
Lightning Source LLC
Chambersburg PA
CBHW061701120626
46550CB00003B/1044